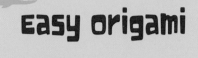
easy origami

EASY OCEAN
Origami

by Christopher L. Harbo

D0317324

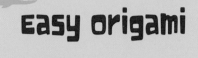

18. JUL 16.
04. SEP 18.

www.raintreepublishers.co.uk
Visit our website to find out
more information about
Raintree books.

To order:
☎ Phone 0845 6044371
🖷 Fax +44 (0) 1865 312263
✉ Email myorders@raintreepublishers.co.uk

Customers from outside the UK please telephone +44 1865 312262

Raintree is an imprint of Capstone Global Library Limited, a company incorporated in England and Wales having its registered office at 7 Pilgrim Street, London, EC4V 6LB – Registered company number: 6695582

First published by Capstone Press in 2011
First published in the United Kingdom in 2012
The moral rights of the proprietor have been asserted.

Photo Credits: Capstone Studio/Karon Dubke, all photos
Artistic Effects: Shutterstock/Klara Viskova, s26,
Seamartini Graphics, SFerdon, stocksock, Z-art
Originated by Capstone Global Library Ltd
Printed and bound in China by Leo Paper Products Ltd

ISBN 978 1 406 24265 2
16 15 14 13 12
10 9 8 7 6 5 4 3 2 1

British Library Cataloguing in Publication Data
A full catalogue record for this book is available from the British Library.

Disclaimer
All the Internet addresses (URLs) given in this book were valid at the time of going to press. However, due to the dynamic nature of the Internet, some addresses may have changed, or sites may have changed or ceased to exist since publication. While the publisher regrets any inconvenience this may cause readers, no responsibility for any such changes can be accepted by the publisher.

ABOUT THE AUTHOR

 Christopher L. Harbo loves origami. He began folding paper several years ago and hasn't stopped. In addition to decorative origami, he also enjoys folding paper aeroplanes. When he's not making origami, Christopher spends his free time reading Japanese comic books and watching films.

TABLE OF
contents

Dive into an origami ocean! This book is overflowing with seven simple models that are all to do with water. Launch a paper ship that really floats. Make a windsurfer that glides with a puff of air. Fold a water lily that blooms in two colours. Don't worry if you've never folded paper before. Now is a great time to test the waters!

MATERIALS

Origami is a simple art that doesn't use many materials. You'll only need the following things to complete the projects in this book:

Origami paper: Square origami paper comes in many fun colours and sizes. You can use 15 by 15 centimetres square paper for the models in this book, unless the instructions tell you to use a different paper size. You can buy this paper in most craft shops.

Clear sticky tape: Most origami models don't need sticky tape. But when they do, you'll be glad that you have it handy.

Scissors: Sometimes a model needs a snip here or there. Keep some scissors near by.

Ruler: Some models use measurements to complete. A ruler will help you measure.

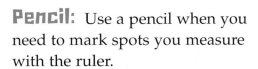

Pencil: Use a pencil when you need to mark spots you measure with the ruler.

Craft supplies: Pens and other craft supplies will help you to decorate your models.

FOLDING TECHNIQUES

Folding paper is easier when you understand basic origami folds and symbols. Practise the folds on this list before trying the models in this book. Turn back to this list if you get stuck on a tricky step, or ask an adult for help.

Valley Folds are represented by a dashed line. One side of the paper is folded against the other like a book. A sharp fold is made by running your finger along the fold line.

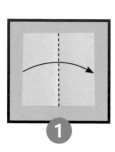

Mountain Folds are represented by a pink or white dashed and dotted line. The paper is folded sharply behind the model.

Squash Folds are formed by lifting one edge of a pocket. The pocket gets folded again so the spine gets flattened. The existing fold lines become new edges.

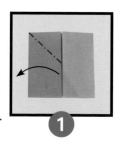

Inside reverse folds are made by opening a pocket slightly. Then you fold the model inside itself along existing fold lines.

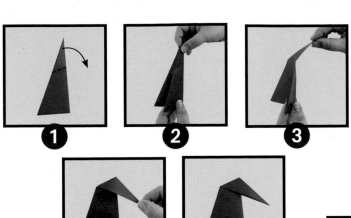

Outside reverse Folds are made by opening a pocket slightly. Then you fold the model outside itself along existing fold lines.

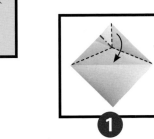

Rabbit ear Folds are formed by bringing two edges of a point together using existing fold lines. The new point is folded to one side.

SYMBOLS

SINGLE-POINTED ARROW:
Fold the paper in the direction of the arrow.

HALF-POINTED ARROW:
Fold the paper behind.

DOUBLE-POINTED ARROW:
Fold the paper and then unfold it.

LOOPING ARROW:
Turn the paper over or turn it to a new position.

ROYAL yacht

Traditional model

Put on your captain's cap and raise a sail! Then imagine speeding across the ocean in this sharp paper yacht.

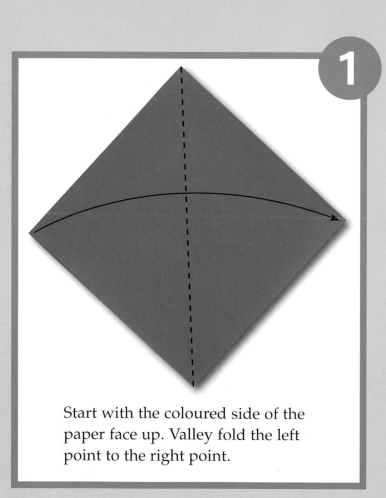

1

Start with the coloured side of the paper face up. Valley fold the left point to the right point.

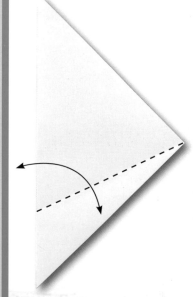

2

Valley fold the bottom point up and to the left. Note how one end of the fold meets the middle point of the triangle. Make a sharp fold and unfold.

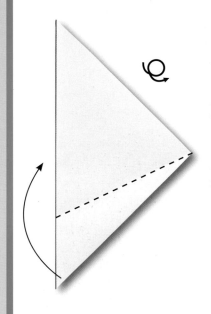

Outside reverse fold the bottom point on the folds from step 2. This fold turns the point inside out. When the fold is complete, turn the model so it points to the left.

4

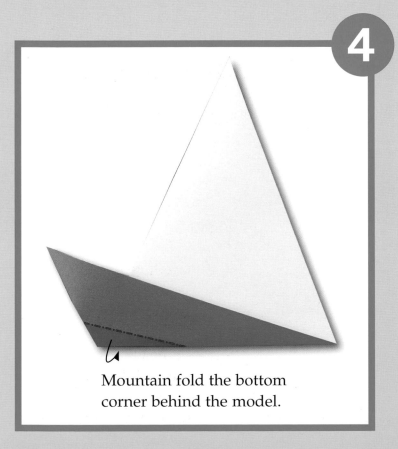

Mountain fold the bottom corner behind the model.

Ahoy there! Your yacht looks fit for the high seas!

5

SECRET tip Use pens or crayons to give your yacht's sail its own style.

FLOATING Ship

Traditional model

Here's a paper ship that really floats! Fold a fleet of ships and set sail on an adventure.

1

Start with the coloured side of the paper face down. Valley fold the bottom-left point to the top-right point.

2

Valley fold the bottom point past the top edge. Note how this fold slants slightly from right to left. Make a sharp fold and unfold.

3

Inside reverse fold the bottom point on the folds from step 2. This fold allows the point to swing up inside the model.

4

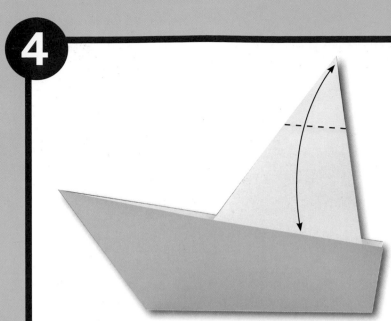

Valley fold the top point to the edge of the top layer. Make a sharp fold and unfold.

5

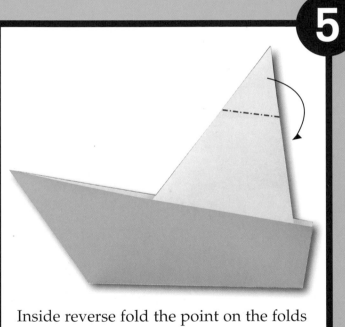

Inside reverse fold the point on the folds from step 4. This fold allows the top point to swing down inside the model.

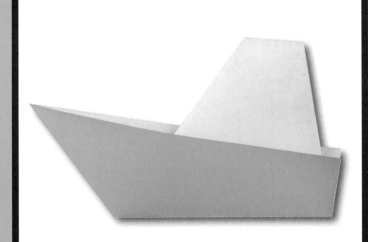

Float your ship in a pond or a kitchen sink.

6

Colour both sides of your ship's bottom edges with a crayon. The crayon wax will protect the edges in the water. Your ship will float longer!

COOL windsurfer

Traditional model

Now you can go windsurfing without ever getting wet! Use a little lung power to send this tiny windsurfer scooting across a table.

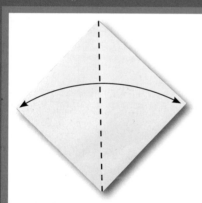

1

Start with the coloured side of the paper face down. Valley fold the left point to the right point and unfold.

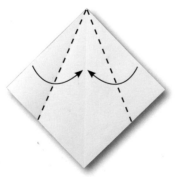

Valley fold the top-left edge to the centre fold. Valley fold the top-right edge to the centre fold.

2

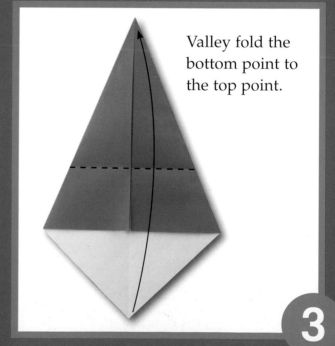

Valley fold the bottom point to the top point.

3

4

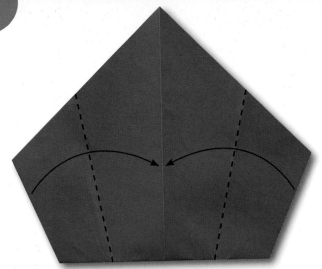

Valley fold the left and right edges to the centre fold.

5

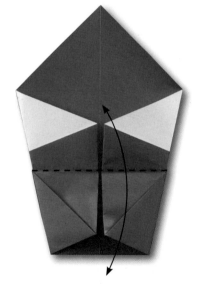

Lift the top layer. Valley fold its point past the bottom edge. This fold connects the slanted edges near the bottom of the model. Make a sharp fold and unfold the point halfway.

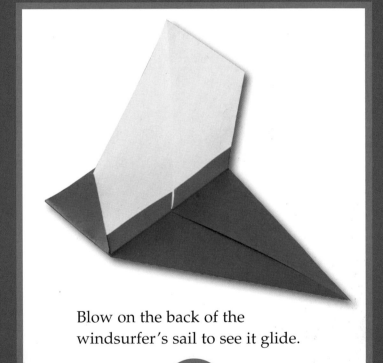

Blow on the back of the windsurfer's sail to see it glide.

6

SECRET tip Make windsurfers for all of your friends. Then hold races to see whose windsurfer is the fastest!

BLUE whale

Traditional model

No animal on Earth is larger than the blue whale.
Find the biggest square of blue paper you can.
Then fold this gentle giant for your origami ocean.

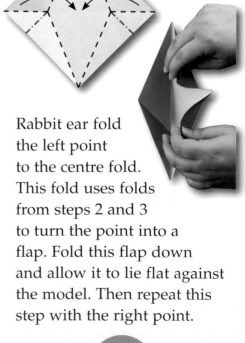

1

Start with the coloured
side of the paper face down.
Valley fold the left point to
the right point and unfold.
Valley fold the top point to
the bottom point and unfold.

2

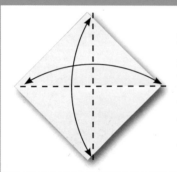

Valley fold the top-left
edge to the centre fold
and unfold. Valley fold
the top-right edge to the
centre fold and unfold.

3

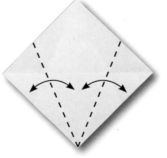

Valley fold the bottom-left
edge to the centre fold and
unfold. Valley fold the
bottom-right edge to the
centre fold and unfold.

4

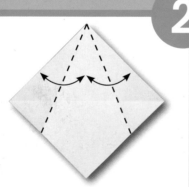

Rabbit ear fold
the left point
to the centre fold.
This fold uses folds
from steps 2 and 3
to turn the point into a
flap. Fold this flap down
and allow it to lie flat against
the model. Then repeat this
step with the right point.

5

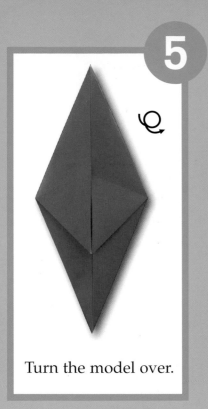

Turn the model over.

6

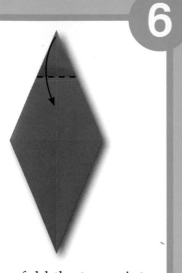

Valley fold the top point. Make this fold about 5 cm from the top of the model.

7

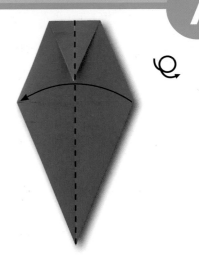

Valley fold the right side of the model to the left. Then turn the model so the head of the whale points to the right.

8

Valley fold the left point. Make this fold slant from left to right so the point sticks straight up. Make a sharp fold and unfold.

9

Inside reverse fold on the folds from step 8. This fold will allow the bottom edge to swing inside the model to make a tail.

10

Draw an underwater scene for your whale.

SECRET tip Tuck a rolled piece of sticky tape inside your whale's body. The tape will hold the two sides of the body together tightly.

15

CLEVER sailboat

Traditional model

Set sail on an origami adventure! This clever sailboat uses both sides of the paper to make two white sails and a coloured hull.

1

Start with the coloured side of the paper face up. Valley fold the bottom-left corner to the top-right corner and unfold. Valley fold the top-left corner to the bottom-right corner and unfold.

2

Turn the paper over.

Valley fold the left edge to the right edge and unfold.

3

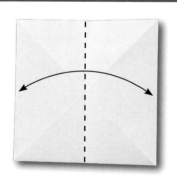

Valley fold the top edge to the bottom edge.

4

Squash fold by lifting the bottom-right corner of the paper. Pull the corner to the left on the existing folds. Flatten the paper into a square shape.

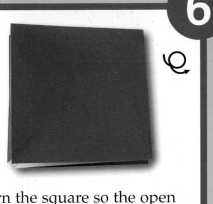

Turn the square so the open end points away from you.

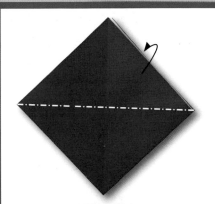

Mountain fold the top point of the top layer inside the model. The point will meet the centre of the paper. Repeat this step on the back side of the model.

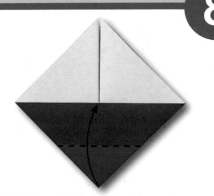

Valley fold the bottom point to the middle edge.

Turn the model over.

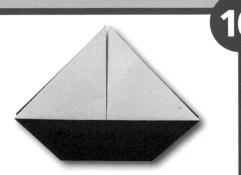

Look, no hands! Your sailboat will stand on its triangle-shaped flap.

SECRET tip To make one sail shorter, mountain fold a sail behind the model. Then valley fold the sail back up. Make this fold a little below the mountain fold. Ta-da! You now have one short sail and one tall sail.

SWImmING goldfish

Traditional model

Fold this model and surprise your friends with a snip, snip, snip. With three simple cuts, you'll turn a samurai helmet into a goldfish.

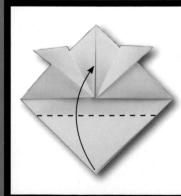

1

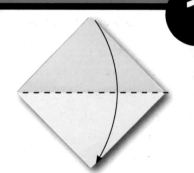

Start with the coloured side of the paper face down. Valley fold the top point to the bottom point.

2

Valley fold the left and right points to the bottom point.

3

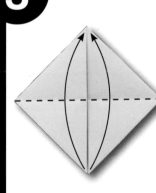

Lift the left side's top layer. Valley fold its bottom point to the top point. Repeat this step on the right side's top layer.

Lift the left side's top layer. Valley fold its top point past the outside edge. Note how the fold meets the centre of the model. Repeat this step on the right side's top layer.

4

Valley fold the top layer of the bottom point. The point should rest about 2·5 cm from the top point.

5

6

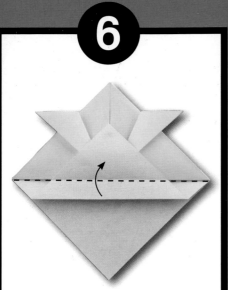

Valley fold the edge made in step 5. The fold runs along the centre edge of the model.

7

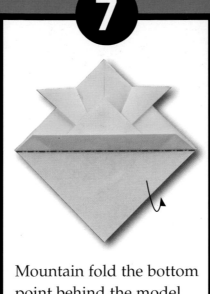

Mountain fold the bottom point behind the model.

8

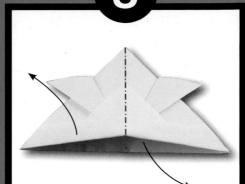

Pull the top and bottom layers of the model apart. Flatten the model completely.

9

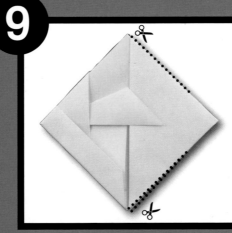

Use scissors to cut along the top-right edge. The cut should end about 1·3 cm from the right corner. Then make similar cuts on both bottom-right edges.

10

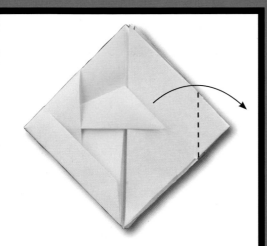

Valley fold the right side's top layer. The fold will connect the ends of the cuts from step 9. Repeat this valley fold on the back side of the model.

11

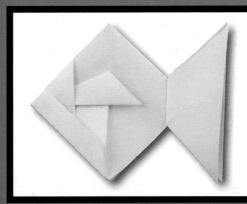

Glub, glub, glub. Your goldfish is ready to swim!

SECRET tip To make a samurai helmet, simply stop after step 7. Place the helmet on a doll's head or make one large enough for you to wear.

WATER lily

Traditional model

Real water lilies only bloom from June to September. But this paper water lily can brighten your day all year long.

1

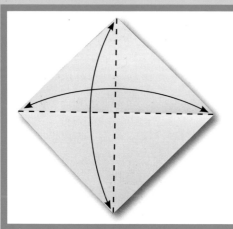

Start with the coloured side of the large paper face down. Valley fold the left point to the right point and unfold. Valley fold the top point to the bottom point and unfold.

2

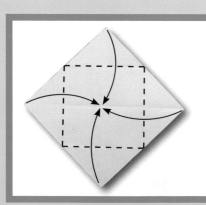

Valley fold all four points to the centre.

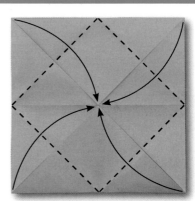

Valley fold all four corners to the centre.

3

SPECIAL note

This model uses two pieces of paper. One piece should be a 25 cm square. The other piece should be a 15 cm square.

4

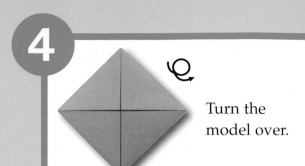

Turn the model over.

5

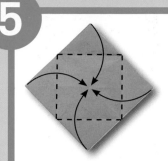

Valley fold all four points to the centre.

6

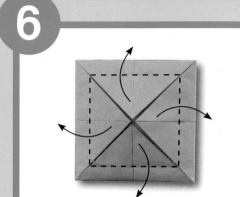

Valley fold all four inside points past the outside edges. Each fold should be about 0·64 cm from the edge.

7

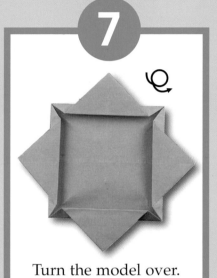

Turn the model over.

8

Lift the four inside points that make up the first layer of the model. Valley fold these points in half and unfold them slightly.

9

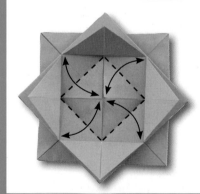

Lift the four inside corners that make up the second layer of the model. Valley fold these corners in half and unfold them slightly.

10

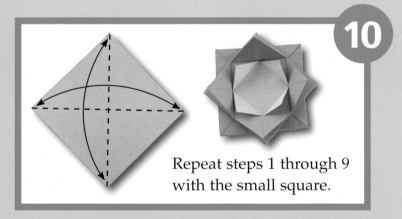

Repeat steps 1 through 9 with the small square.

11

Place the bottom corners of the small blossom into the centre of the larger blossom.

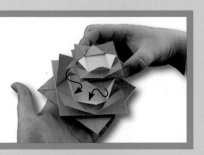

12

Your water lily is blooming!

Origami
OCEAN FUN

READ more

My First Origami Book: Things That Go, Nick Robinson (Dover Publications, 2012)

Origami for Children, Mari Ono and Roshin Ono (Cico, 2008)

Origami Ooh La La!: Origami for Performance and Play, Jeremy Shafer (Createspace, 2010)

Origami Zoo: An Amazing Collection of Folded Paper Animals, Robert J. Lang (St. Martin's Griffin, 2006)

INTERNET sites

You can find other interesting origami models on the websites below, along with step-by-step guides on how to make each model.

www.activityvillage.co.uk/origami_for_kids.htm

www.enchantedlearning.com/crafts/origami/